Aviation Radio Communications Made Easy

VFR Edition

Aviation Radio Communications Made Easy

VFR Edition

Talk like a pro with templates
that function as a script for your VFR flights

by Hugh C. Ward, Jr., Ed.D.

Aviation Supplies & Academics, Inc.
7005 132nd Place SE
Newcastle, Washington 98059
www.asa2fly.com

Aviation Radio Communications Made Easy, VFR Edition
by Hugh C. Ward, Jr., Ed.D.

Aviation Supplies & Academics, Inc.
7005 132nd Place SE
Newcastle, Washington 98059-3153

Email: asa@asa2fly.com
Web: www.asa2fly.com

Published 2005 by Aviation Supplies & Academics, Inc.

Printed in the United States of America

08   07   06   05   9   8   7   6   5   4   3   2   1

ASA-COMM-VFR
ISBN   1-56027-584-7
         978-1-56027-584-8

08

Contents

Continued

Note 1   The reverse side of each template includes a grid for easy note-taking and quick calculations.

Note 2   There are four (4) copies included for templates VFR • 1 through VFR • 29, and two (2) copies for templates VFR • 30, VFR • 31 and VFR • 32.

How to Use This Book

Student Pilots

This book will support student pilots' efforts to understand what to say and when to say it during a flight. By constructing a VFR communication "script" during their preflight and then using the "script" in flight, students are better prepared mentally to accomplish, in a quick and accurate manner, the necessary communication exchanges. Enough copies of the communication templates are included to support the student pilots through each of the required cross-country flights necessary to secure a private pilot's license.

Inactive Pilots

The old adage, "If you don't use it, you lose it!" is particularly appropriate when applied to the inactive pilot. Safe aviation communications require the pilot to listen and understand ATC clearances and instructions, and respond in a quick and accurate manner. Aviation communications also calls for the pilot to see the "communication big picture." Without timely practice, the inactive pilot loses sight of the "communication big picture" rapidly, and it is not easy to regain. When the inactive pilot prepares a VFR communication script during preflight, the pieces of the big picture start coming back together again. Using the VFR templates to construct VFR communication scripts for several flights will help the inactive pilot regain the "communication big picture" quickly and with less anxiety and stress.

Active Pilots

Active pilots know, understand, and use VFR communication protocols effectively. The cockpit, however, is a busy place during a cross-country flight. Selecting, sequencing, and partially completing a set of the book's templates to match an upcoming cross-country flight during the preflight reduces the workload in the cockpit during flight. By using this unique communication "memory aid," the active pilot gains "think time" for other matters he or she may encounter during the cross-country. A prepared pilot is a focused pilot.

Flight Instructors

A CFI's first love is teaching the student pilot how to fly an airplane. Because the skills necessary to fly an airplane are largely kinesthetic in nature, most CFIs find this portion of the student pilot training to be intuitive and relatively easy to do. Teaching the student pilot how to communicate, however, requires the CFI to constantly explain, and re-explain, the various pieces of the "communication big picture." For those students who have a mental block about communications, competency can be an especially frustrating, time consuming, and expensive task. Some students quit after encountering trouble with communications! When the CFI helps the student select, sequence, and partially complete a set of the book's templates to match an upcoming cross-country flight during the preflight, the CFI helps lower the anxiety and stress levels of the student. Reducing the student's anxiety and stress level decreases the CFI's need to coach the student during inflight communications. Nothing builds confidence more than a successful cross-country flight. In short, use of the templates in this book makes VFR communications instruction easier on everyone involved.

Ground School Instructors

Whether ground schools are conducted with small groups of pilots in rather informal settings, or with large groups of pilots in formal settings, teaching the airspace and communication portion of the curriculum can be challenging. Helping students visualize the airspace system and the necessary communications required in each type of airspace near and away from an airport can be time consuming. Because ground schools are run for a set number of hours a week over a limited number of weeks, ground school instructors cannot spend a large amount of time on any one topic. Using the book's templates, template descriptions, and other supporting information helps shorten the amount of time necessary to explain airspace and VFR communication topics.

Students are shown how to construct a hypothetical VFR communication script from one airport to another airport using the templates from the book. The students are then given different departure and destination airports and are asked to construct the correct communication sequence on their own. Attention ground school instructors: After this exercise, the student's CFI will love you!

Students Who Speak English as a Second Language

Learning a second language is a difficult and time-consuming task. Aviation communications in a second language is an especially difficult task. Use of these templates will give the English-as-a-second-language student the correct sentence structure to speak the communications critical to safe flying.

A Final Note

Aviation Radio Communications Made Easy, VFR Edition is a versatile product that can be used as a memory aid, training tool, confidence builder, classroom exercise workbook, and much more!

Script Assembly Instructions

Since complex aviation communications are consistent and predictable, they follow a known formula based on your location and intent (departure, en route, approach). Once you understand these scenarios, you will be able to anticipate communications and respond accordingly. The templates in this book allow VFR pilots to construct a unique communication script for every VFR flight, regardless of its complexity or the number of communications required, to practice these scenarios to perfection.

Complete the following five steps to prepare for your next VFR flight:

1. **Identify** the types of airspace that surround your starting airport, your route, all landing airports enroute, and your final destination airport.
2. **Determine** what types of communications will most likely occur entering and exiting each airspace. *See* Table 1 on the next page.
3. **Take out** the necessary blank templates that match your flight plan and assemble them in the correct sequence.
4. **Fill in** as much information on each template as you can before departing.
5. **Practice** your "communication script" before departure.

There will be times when the next communication from ATC will require you to do a "readback." The templates are set up as complete sentences. Just fill in the blanks with the information supplied by ATC on the template and do a quick "readback." If you have practiced your script several times, then the script's templates will quickly become like notecards for a speech.

At each point in your flight where a communication is required, you should quickly refer to the appropriate template in your communication script before speaking. All you need to do to stay on track during flight is turn over the template pages with each communication. After a few flights your "delivery" of the expected communication will get smoother and quicker. *It just takes practice.*

VFR Communications Template Guide

		Airspace				
		G	**E**	**D**	**C**	**B**
Approaching Airport	AWOS	✔*				
	ATIS		✔	✔	✔	✔
	Approach Control			✔	✔	✔
	Control Tower		✔*	✔	✔	✔
	Ground Control			✔	✔	✔
	Announce Landing Intentions	✔	✔			
Departing Airport	AWOS	✔*	✔*			
	Announce Takeoff Intentions	✔	✔			
	ATIS			✔	✔	✔
	Clearance Delivery			✔	✔	✔
	Ground Control			✔*	✔*	✔
	Control Tower		✔*	✔	✔	✔
	Departure Control			✔	✔	✔

* if available

Please note: ATC services at specific airports may be combined or may not be available at certain times. Determine the approximate times you will be approaching or departing the airports you will be using. Check a current copy of the *Airport/Facility Directory* to confirm which ATC services may be available.

Table 1

VFR Template Descriptions and Tips

VFR • 1   Flight Route

Allows the pilot to layout the general route sequence with appropriate notes. For example, if the pilot will be passing over a location where a NOTAM has been issued, a notation may be helpful.

VFR • 2   Takeoff Nontowered Airport

At a nontowered airport, announcing your directions for departure taxi, runway, and general flight path intentions is critical to a safe "see and avoid" policy. Be aware that some airports have "calm wind" or preferred runways. Check your A/FD or contact CTAF or UNICOM for the latest runway preferences.

VFR • 3   Initial Nontowered Airport Contact/Response

At a nontowered airport, announcing your presence and general location alerts pilots in the pattern that another plane is near. This communication is critical to a safe "see and avoid" policy. Knowing the wind at the destination airport before you arrive allows you time to mentally map your approach to the airport. Use the blank space on the template to actually draw a simple sketch.

VFR • 4   Entering Nontowered Airport Landing Pattern Intentions

At a nontowered airport, announcing your approach, landing pattern, and runway use intentions is critical to a safe "see and avoid" policy. Don't forget to call each left or right traffic leg of your landing pattern. Announcing your departure from the active runway onto a taxiway after landing helps pilots still in the pattern, and other taxiing aircraft, know your location.

VFR • 5   Set VOR

While this template is not actually for a communications procedure, setting your VOR to the correct value is critical to safe
VFR navigation. VOR (VHF Omni-directional Range) is a tried
and true navigation service and is the tool of choice for VFR
pilots without a GPS. Use the compass rose image to help
layout your position relative to the VOR source. This template
should help with "reverse sensing." On a long cross-country
flight, you may need to use several of these templates.

VFR • 6   Activate Flight Plan

After filing a flight plan, you should activate it just before
departure by calling Flight Service at 1.800.WX.BRIEF or from
the air just after takeoff. Having an active flight plan ensures
that someone will come looking for you if you have to make an
emergency landing. Don't forget to close your flight plan!

VFR • 7   Close Flight Plan

In certain situations closing your flight plan on the ground is
impractical. This template allows you to close it from the air. In
any case, you must close your flight plan no more than 30
minutes beyond your stated time of arrival. If you do not,
various federal, state, and local agencies will start looking
for you.

Lots of taxpayers' money each year is spent tracking down
(Pardon the pun!) safely-landed aircraft.

VFR • 8   Acquire ATIS, ASOS, or AWOS

ATIS (Automatic Terminal Information Service), AWOS (Automated Weather Observation System), and ASOS (Automated
Surface Observation System) broadcast a recorded message
containing information such as runways in use, altimeter
setting, weather conditions, wind direction and velocity, and
other information pertinent to operating in the vicinity of or on
the airport. Pay particular attention to "Land and Hold Short

Operations" (LAHSO) instructions. ATIS is the service used at controlled airports. You will encounter ASOS or AWOS mostly at nontowered airports.

Whenever the weather or other conditions change during the day, the recording is updated. Each time the ATIS recording is updated, it is assigned an identifier name, starting with ALPHA. Subsequent updates are identified as BRAVO, CHARLIE, etc. When making initial contact with Approach Control or Tower on arrival, and Clearance Delivery or Ground Control on departure, you should state that you have the current ATIS information by name; e.g., "I have information Tango."

VFR • 9 Initial Approach Control Contact

Contact with Approach Control is mandatory prior to entry into Class B (within 20 miles) and Class C airspace. Your initial contact should identify who you are calling, the type and registration number of your aircraft, your approximate position and altitude relative to your destination airport, and your requests. This strategy is commonly called the **Who, Who, Where, What procedure**. This communication is crucial so be prepared.

VFR • 10 Initial Approach Control Class B Response

Since this is Class B airspace, you must get actual clearance from ATC to enter.

VFR • 11 Initial Approach Control Class C Response

The controller may respond with a "SQUAWK" code for your transponder. While you are entering the SQUAWK code, repeat it back to Approach Control. You may also be asked to "IDENT."

Once Approach Control "sees you" on his screen, you will get heading and altitude instructions to bring you into a runway landing pattern.

Please Note: Because a working transponder is the key to your entry into Class B or C airspace, always test your transponder on the ground before takeoff.

VFR • 12 Initial Controlled Airport Contact/ Response After Using Approach Control

The time between Approach Control contact and your initial Tower contact may be several minutes. Do not become nervous. Approach Control will inform you when you are being "handed over" to the Tower and when you should make contact. Most of the time, the initial Tower instructions will be very similar to Approach Control's directions with only the "cleared for landing" statement being added.

Caution: Whenever in doubt about ATC instructions, ask for a repeat, i.e., "Say again, please."

VFR • 13 Initial Controlled Airport Without an Approach Control Contact

Use whatever local flight service reports are available, such as ATIS, AWOS, or ASOS, before you call. Knowing the wind direction and speed at the destination airport, **before** you arrive, allows you time to mentally map out your approach to the airport. Most airports, without a separate Approach and Departure Control, have Class E or D airspace surrounding them. Contact with the Tower is necessary prior to entry into the controlled airspace surrounding an airport. Your initial contact should identify who you are calling, the type and registration number of your aircraft, your approximate position and altitude relative to your destination airport, and your requests. This strategy is commonly called the **Who, Who, Where, What procedure**. This communication is crucial so be prepared!

VFR • 14 Initial Controlled Airport Without an Approach Control Response

Knowing the landing patterns that can be expected at an airport really helps with anticipating what ATC will say to you. The *Airport/Facility Directory* is a great help here. In response to your request for landing instructions, most of the time the Tower will give you pattern and runway directions. Finally, listen very carefully for the "clear to land" phrase. Ask again, if you don't hear it. Watch for light signals from the tower, if your radio goes out. Use template **VFR • 31 Communications Without a Radio**.

VFR • 15 Ground Control Taxi After Landing Request

Look over an airport map of your destination to become familiar with the taxiway locations and names **before** you depart. When you depart the runway after you land, you don't want to tie up the Ground Control frequency asking the question, "Hey, where am I?" If you are at an unfamiliar airport, you may wish to request "progressive" taxi instructions. Finally, remember that FAA does not allow ATC to pick an FBO. Be prepared to ask for one specifically by name.

VFR • 16 Clearance Delivery Contact

At larger airports which have a high volume of operations, Clearance Delivery provides initial departure information to the pilot and frees Ground Control to concentrate on directing traffic on the ramps and taxiways. Clearance Delivery coordinates information with Departure Control by assigning a transponder code prior to takeoff. This departure information saves time both for the Ground Controller and the Departure Controller. This departure information from Clearance Delivery also allows the pilot to set-up the transponder and departure frequencies prior to departure, as well as giving the pilot advance information on departure procedures.

VFR • 17 Clearance Delivery Response

Almost certainly, you will be given a SQUAWK code. Be prepared to immediately dial the code and orally "read" the code back. If you are unsure of the code, ask for a repeat. Remember that once you get a code, you are "tagged" as a departing flight and therefore Departure Control knows about you.

VFR • 18 Ground Control Contact When Ready to Depart

When you initially call, identify your aircraft type and registration number, your precise location on the airport, and a request to taxi to the active runway. Finally, declare your desired general direction of flight.

Study the airport map before you call to see which taxiway leads you to which runway and to know the taxiway names. If you are at an unfamiliar airport, you may wish to request "progressive" taxi instructions.

VFR • 19 Ground Control Response to Your Departure Request

Once Ground Control "sees" you, follow the directions to your active runway explicitly. Even on the ground, follow the "see and avoid" policy. Be vigilant at all runway and taxiways intersections regardless of clearances.

Whenever in doubt, prior to crossing a taxiway or runway, about whether or not you have permission to cross—**ASK!**

VFR • 20 Ground Control Providing Clearance Delivery Contact When Ready to Depart

At most small controlled airports, Clearance Delivery is combined with Ground Control. When you use this template, be sure to include the current ATIS identifier in your initial call-up. Be sure to use the template **VFR • 19 Ground Control Response to Your Departure Request** to write down Ground Control's instructions.

VFR • 21 Tower Contact When Ready to Depart

Once you are at the intersection of the designated taxiway and your designated departure runway, *and you are ready to depart*, contact the Tower and announce your desire to depart.

VFR • 22 Tower Response to Your Departure Request

Be patient about getting a response. Placing you on the active runway just after a landed airplane or just before an approaching airplane on final is a very critical decision for ATC. They want to be sure all aircraft are safely separated. However, if you have not heard from them after three or four minutes, give them another call-up (tactfully).

VFR • 23 Initial Departure Control Contact

Departure Control is a Radar Service at Class B and a number of Class C airports. To operate in this environment, you must be equipped with a Mode C (altitude reporting) transponder. The Departure Controller will assign altitudes and headings as required to provide traffic separation. Soon after takeoff, the tower will tell you to contact Departure Control on a specified frequency for further instructions.

VFR • 24 Initial Departure Control Response

Departure Control's response will be to direct your departure from the airport's controlled airspace in the general direction and altitude close to the ones you requested. Once at the edge of the controlled airspace surrounding the airport, you will be contacted and told to "resume your own navigation." This does not mean radar services are automatically terminated. Continue using your current transponder code unless provided a new one. Most of the time, however, you will be told to change to 1200.

VFR • 25 Transit MOA or Restricted Area Contact

Crossing MOAs is allowed without contacting the controlling center based upon complying with altitude and transition times restrictions found in a current sectional map. Consider contacting the controlling center anyway for any special conditions that may exist. Contact the controlling center **before** you begin to cross an MOA.

As for restricted areas, you **must** contact the controlling center to request permission to cross.

VFR • 26 Transit MOA or Restricted Area Response

The controlling center or approach will advise you if the area(s) you wish to transit is/are "**Hot**" (active) or "**Cold**" (inactive). If you decide to cross after getting a "**Cold**" indication, keep listening for area status updates until you leave the MOA and restricted area(s).

VFR • 27 Flight Following Contact

Whenever you are on a cross-country flight, an extra pair of eyes watching out for other air traffic and what type of airspace you are transitioning can be very helpful. Approach Control will provide "these extra eyes" for VFR pilots, **if their workload permits**. They will point out potential flight conflicts relative to your position. Here is an example: suppose you are flying on heading 90 at 1,500 feet MSL and another aircraft is flying on heading 180 at 1,500 ft. MSL. Now suppose the other aircraft is currently about 10 miles from you at a bearing of 45 degrees (out your left front window.) Approach Control would advise you of the potential conflict and may suggest a course of action. Here is what they may say, *"STAR 12345, traffic at 10 o'clock at your altitude 10 miles heading south. Suggest heading change to 45° until notified."* You should respond to Approach Control's information with your aircraft's make and tail number and an acknowledgment. For example, *"Wardville Approach Control, STAR 12345, roger last plane contact heading south at my attitude, turning to heading 45°."*

VFR • 28 Flight Following Response

The biggest problem for you will be having a sense of where the traffic is. Use the "airplane clock" to easily mark their positions.

VFR • 29 General Purpose Communication Template

This template follows the **Who, Who, Where, What** aviation communications protocol. This basic format is generally accepted for most communication necessary between an aircraft and the control tower, an aircraft and another aircraft in the air and/or on the ground. The template is flexible enough for the vast majority aviation communication needs of proficient pilots. It is very useful for new pilots when odd circumstances occur which require some structure such as an announcement of location, i.e., "abeam the numbers," request of the tower, i.e., "extended landing," etc. Every cross-country communications script should have one or two of these templates included.

VFR • 30 Communication Tips

To master the aviation pronouncement system, listen to communications at local airports whenever you get a chance. You may be surprised how quickly you pick it up. In the meantime, refer to this card when you need help "talking the talk"— aviation style.

VFR • 31 Communications Without a Radio

This template lists the light signals ATC will flash at you if you lose radio communications (often referred to as NORDO operations). In the case of a partial radio breakdown, you may be asked to "IDENT," followed by light signals. If you are using two frequencies to communicate, watch out for "cross channeling." To reduce the chance of being in any of these positions, do a radio check before every flight.

VFR • 32 Emergency Communications

Just think, "*Hey, I can do this!*" Then just do it!

1. **Stay calm**.
2. **Aviate.** Get your plane into a best glide attitude.
3. **Navigate.** Look for the best place to land.
4. **Communicate.** Let someone know where you are!

Tune your transponder to one of the following:

7700 for an engine out or some other form of mechanical problem

   or

7600 for a radio out

   or

7500 for a hijacking.

Sample Flight Script

What follows is an example of the suggested VFR communications templates in the correct sequence for a hypothetical flight. This hypothetical flight originates from the Class G airport at DeLand, Florida (DED), and goes directly through Class E airspace to the Class D airport at Craig Field in Jacksonville, Florida (CRG). This Sample Flight ends in an area with heavy military and commercial traffic. Therefore, communication with the local control center (Steps 6 and 7) is considered a prudent, though not required, step.

Flight Route

Date ...... *October 13, 2004* ....

Time ...... *3:00 p.m.* ....

From ...... *DED* ....

To ...... *Craig* ....

To ...... *Heading 350* ....

To ....

To ....

To ....

To ....

To ....

Takeoff Nontowered Airport

122.8 • " DeLand .... **traffic**
.... Frequency .... Airport Name/City

STAR 12345 .... **departing runway** 5
.... *Who:* Make and Tail # ....

to the North • DeLand "
.... N, S, E, W .... Airport Name/City .

VFR • 2
SAMPLE

Use the area below to map out your ramp–to–takeoff–runway path.

5

SET VOR

.... *Craig* .... **VOR**

Airport Name/City

.... *114.5* .... **Frequency**

Transmit and Receive

.... • .... **Frequency**

Transmit only   Receive only

Set ("TO") or "FROM" .... *350* ....

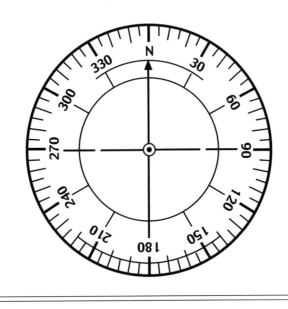

Activate Flight Plan

Tune radio to .... *122.4* • *St. Petersburg* ....
Frequency Airport Name/City

OR

FSS telephone number ..... *1.800.WX.BRIEF* ......

Pilot says:

" *St. Petersburg* **radio** *STAR 12345*
Airport Name/City Who: Make and Tail #

listening on ... *122.4* ... **at** ... *Ormond* ... (VOR) **or RCO.** "
Frequency Location

VFR • 6
SAMPLE

Flight Service Response:

" **Go ahead** ...... *STAR 12345* ...... "
Who: Make and Tail #

Pilot Response:

" ...... *St. Petersburg* ...... **radio, I wish to open**
Airport Name/City

my flight plan from ...... *DeLand* ......

to ...... *Craig* ...... **and to** .... "
Optional

Acquire ATIS, AWOS, or ASOS

125.4   (ATIS,) AWOS, or ASOS   _Craig_
Frequency   Airport Name/City

19:53Z • 330, 10 • 23, 18
Time   Wind: Dir/Speed/Gust   Temp/Dew

Clear below 12
Sky Conditions

30.10 • 32 •
Altimeter   Rwy(s) in Use   Rwy Freq.(s)

• PAPA
Density Altitude   Information Letter

birds north end
Additional Information

NOTAMs

Initial Approach Control Contact

Frequency ...... *127.0* ...... North Approach

Frequency ...... (*120.75*) ...... South Approach

Frequency ...... *118.6* ...... East Approach

Frequency ...... West Approach

Frequency ...... *119.0* ...... • ...... Approach
(NW,) NE, SW, SE

" ...... *JAX* ...... approach ...... *STAR 12345* ......
Airport Name/City   Who: Make and Tail #

...... *20 miles* ...... • ...... *South* ...... at ...... *1,500* ...... feet
Where: Distance   Direction   Altitude MSL

inbound for ......
What: Stop and Go, (Full Stop Landing,) etc.

at ...... *Craig* ....
Optional: Satellite Airport Name/City

with information ...... *PAPA* ...... " .
ATIS: Letter

......
Additional Information

Initial Approach Control
Class C Response

"Squawk ..... *1315* ..... and (IDENT)"
Optional

"(Maintain) current heading."

__OR__

"Turn ..... to heading ..... ."
L/R

__AND/OR__

"(Maintain.) descend to, or ascend to ..... *1,500* ..... feet

for entering ..... *L* ..... • ..... *BASE* .....
L/R   Pattern Leg

for runway ..... *32* ..... ."

__AND/OR__

"Contact Tower at ..... *132.1* ..... when
Frequency

..... *5* ..... miles from the ..... *airport* ..... ."
Airport, Midfield Downwind, etc.

Close Flight Plan

Tune radio to ...... *122.45* ...... ● ...... *Gainesville* ......
                     Frequency   Airport Name/City

OR

FSS telephone number ...... *1.800.WX.BRIEF* ......

Pilot says:

" ...... *Gainesville* ...... **radio** ...... *STAR 12345* ......
           Airport Name/City   Who: Make and Tail #

listening on ...... *122.45* ...... **at** ...... *Ormond* ...... (VOR) **or RCO.** "
                  Frequency   Location

Flight Service Response:

"Go ahead ...... *STAR 12345* ...... "
                               Who: Make and Tail #

Pilot Response:

" ...... *Gainesville* ...... **radio, I wish to close my**
               Airport Name/City

flight plan from ...... *DeLand* ......

to ...... *Craig* ......

and to .... **I have the airport in sight.** "
               Optional

VFR • 7 SAMPLE

Initial Tower Contact / Response
After Using Approach Control

VFR • 12
SAMPLE

.... • .... •
Frequency   Runway

_132.1_ • .... • _Craig_ ....
Frequency   Runway   Airport Name/City

" _Craig_ .... **tower** _STAR 12345_ •
    Airport Name/City   *Who:* Make and Tail #

_5_ • _South_ **at** _1,500_ **feet**
Where: Distance   Direction   Altitude

Necessary for Class D, optional for Class B or Class C airspace:

inbound for entering _L_ • _BASE_ ....
                     L/R   Pattern Leg

for runway _32_ ....

"
for ....
          Option: (Full Stop Landing) Touch and Go, etc.

Tower Response:

" _STAR 12345_ .... **cleared for** _L_ ....
       Who: Make and Tail #   L/R

BASE **landing on runway** _32_ "
    Pattern Leg

Or " ....

Ground Control Taxi After Landing Request

<u>121.80</u>   **•**   <u>Craig</u>
Frequency   Airport Name/City

" <u>Craig</u> **Ground Control**
Airport Name/City

<u>STAR 12345</u>

Who: Make and Tail #

at <u>32</u> **and** <u>BRAVO</u>
Runway   Taxiway

requests .... **taxi**

(Direct,) Progressive

instructions to <u>west ramp</u> **"** .
FBO or airport location

Use the area below to map out the taxi path to your final stop on the airport grounds.

Communication Tips

Tip 1 The following format is generally used at initial call-up:

    1. **WHO** you are calling.
    2. **WHO** you are.
    3. **WHERE** you are.
    4. **WHAT** you want or what you are doing.

Tip 2 Be sure to pronounce numbers and letters correctly. Speak each word distinctly, at a speech rate of about 100 words a minute. Use the table below as a guide.

0 ....Zero	A .... Alpha	N .... November
1 .... One	B .... Bravo	O .... October
2 .... Two	C ....Charlie	P .... Papa
3 ....Tree	D .... Delta	Q .... Quebec
4 .... Fore	E .... Echo	R ....Romeo
5 ....Fife	F .... Foxtrot	S .... Sierra
6 ....Six	G .... Golf	T .... Tango
7 .... Seven	H .... Hotel	U .... Uniform
8 .... Eight	I .... India	V ....Victor
9 .... Nin-er	J .... Juliet	W ...... Whiskey
	K .... Kilo	X .... X-Ray
	L ....Lima	Y .... Yankee
	M .... Mike	Z .... Zulu

Tip 3 When pronouncing numbers, use the digit format for numbers less than four digits, and the group format for numbers with four or more.

Examples

    93 is said *Nin-er Tree*
    138 is said *One Tree Eight*
    9500 is said *Nin-er Thousand Fife Hundred*
    1050 is said *One Thousand Fifty* or *Ten Fifty*
    14500 is said *One Four Thousand Fife Hundred*

Communications Without a Radio

In the air:
1. Squawk 7600 (loss of radio) on your transponder.
2. Determine the airport landing patterns.
3. Enter the pattern at a 45° angle to the downwind leg.
4. Turn on your navigation and beacon lights.
5a. **Daytime:** Rock your wings and watch for the Tower's light signals.
5b. **Nighttime:** Flash landing lights and watch for the Tower's light signals.

On the ground:
1. Watch for other taxing aircraft.
2. Flash landing lights.
3. Watch for the Tower's light signals.

Color and Type of Signal	On The Gound	In Flight
	Meaning	
Steady Green	Cleared for takeoff	Cleared to land
Flashing Green	Cleared to taxi	Return for landing (to be followed by a steady green at proper time)
Steady Red	STOP!	Give way to other aircraft and continue circling
Flashing Red	Taxi clear of the landing area (runway) in use	Airport unsafe! DO NOT LAND!
Flashing White	Return to your starting point on airport	No assigned meaning
Alternating Red and Green	Exercise extreme caution	Exercise extreme caution

Emergency Communications

Stay calm.
Aviate • Navigate • Communicate

1. **Set** your transponder to:
   - 7700 for a mechanical, powerplant or electrical problem,
   - 7600 for a radio problem,
   - 7500 for a hijacking situation.

2. **Set** your radio to the emergency frequency **121.5** or
   call on your current frequency ....

3. **Say** "**Mayday, Mayday, Mayday**.

_____ *STAR 12345* _____
Who: Make and Tail #

.... **miles** ....
       Number   *Where:* N, S, E, W

of ....
                             Location, Landmark, or Checkpoint

with .... **souls on board at** .... **feet**
         Number   Altitude MSL

"

....
                             Problem

Flight Route

Date ....

Time ....

From ....

To ....

To ....

To ....

To ....

To ....

To ....

To ....

Sectional Scale 1:500,000	10 Nautical Miles			
10 Statute Miles				

Flight Route

Date ....

Time ....

From ....

To ....

To ....

To ....

To ....

To ....

To ....

To ....

Sectional Scale 1:500,000	10 Nautical Miles			
10 Statute Miles				

Flight Route

Date ....

Time ....

From ....

To ....

To ....

To ....

To ....

To ....

To ....

To ....

Sectional Scale 1:500,000	10 Nautical Miles			
10 Statute Miles				

Flight Route

Date ....

Time ....

From ....

To ....

To ....

To ....

To ....

To ....

To ....

To ....

Sectional Scale 1:500,000	10 Nautical Miles			
10 Statute Miles				

Takeoff Nontowered Airport

.... • " .... traffic

Frequency   Airport Name/City

.... departing runway ....

Who: Make and Tail #

to the .... • ....

N, S, E, W   Airport Name/City

Use the area below to map out your ramp–to–takeoff–runway path.

Sectional Scale 1:500,000	10 Nautical Miles			
10 Statute Miles				

Takeoff Nontowered Airport

.... • " .... **traffic**
Frequency   Airport Name/City

.... **departing runway** ....
Who: Make and Tail #

to the .... • .... "
N, S, E, W   Airport Name/City

Use the area below to map out your ramp-to-takeoff-runway path.

Sectional Scale 1:500,000	10 Nautical Miles			
10 Statute Miles				

Takeoff Nontowered Airport

.... • " .... **traffic**
    Frequency   Airport Name/City

.... **departing runway** ....
  Who: Make and Tail #

to the .... • ....
    N, S, E, W   Airport Name/City

Use the area below to map out your ramp–to–takeoff–runway path.

Sectional Scale 1:500,000	10 Nautical Miles			
10 Statute Miles				

Takeoff Nontowered Airport

VFR·2

.... • " .... **traffic**

Frequency   Airport Name/City

.... **departing runway** ....

Who: Make and Tail #

to the .... • .... "

N, S, E, W   Airport Name/City

Use the area below to map out your ramp–to–takeoff–runway path.

Sectional Scale 1:500,000	10 Nautical Miles				
10 Statute Miles					

Initial Nontowered Airport Contact/Response

.... • ....
Frequency   Airport Name/City

"
.... **traffic** .... •
Airport Name/City UNICOM   *Who:* Make and Tail #

.... • .... **at** .... **feet**
Where: Distance   Direction   Altitude

inbound for ....
                    What: Stop and Go, Full Stop Landing, etc.

Statement Choices:

...requests an airport advisory?"

OR

...what is the favored runway?"

Probable response information:

....
Runway in Use

....
Wind Direction/Speed

....
Special Conditions

VFR • 3

Sectional Scale 1:500,000	10 Nautical Miles			
10 Statute Miles				

Initial Nontowered Airport Contact/Response

.... • ....

Frequency   Airport Name/City

" .... traffic .... •

Airport Name/City   UNICOM   *Who:* Make and Tail #

.... • .... at .... feet

Where: Distance   Direction   Altitude

inbound for ....

What: Stop and Go, Full Stop Landing, etc.

Statement Choices:

...requests an airport advisory?"

—
OR
—

...what is the favored runway?"

Probable response information:

....

Runway in Use

....

Wind Direction/Speed

....

Special Conditions

Sectional Scale 1:500,000	10 Nautical Miles			
10 Statute Miles				

Initial Nontowered Airport Contact/Response

.... • ....
Frequency   Airport Name/City

" .... **traffic** .... •
Airport Name/City UNICOM   *Who:* Make and Tail #

.... • .... **at** .... **feet**
Where: Distance   Direction   Altitude

inbound for ....
                  What: Stop and Go, Full Stop Landing, etc.

Statement Choices:

...requests an airport advisory?"

—
OR
—

...what is the favored runway?"

Probable response information:

....
Runway in Use

....
Wind Direction/Speed

....
Special Conditions

Sectional Scale 1:500,000	10 Nautical Miles			
10 Statute Miles				

Initial Nontowered Airport Contact/Response

.... • ....
 Frequency   Airport Name/City

" .... **traffic** .... •
 Airport Name/City UNICOM   *Who:* Make and Tail #

.... • .... **at** .... **feet**
 Where: Distance   Direction   Altitude

inbound for ....
               What: Stop and Go, Full Stop Landing, etc.

Statement Choices:

...requests an airport advisory?"

—
OR
—

...what is the favored runway?"

Probable response information:

....
                          Runway in Use

....
                     Wind Direction/Speed

....
                       Special Conditions

Sectional Scale 1:500,000	10 Nautical Miles			
10 Statute Miles				

Entering Nontowered Airport Landing Pattern Intentions

" .... • traffic ....
Airport Name/City   UNICOM   *Who:* Make and Tail #

entering .... • ....
             L/R   Pattern Leg

at .... feet • for runway .... "
Altitude MSL or "Pattern Altitude"

VFR • 4

Use the area below to map out your landing pattern legs.

Sectional Scale 1:500,000	10 Nautical Miles			
10 Statute Miles				

Entering Nontowered Airport Landing Pattern Intentions

"
.... • **traffic** ....
Airport Name/City   UNICOM   *Who:* Make and Tail #

entering .... • ....
                L/R   Pattern Leg

at .... **feet** • **for runway** ...."
Altitude MSL or "Pattern Altitude"

Use the area below to map out your landing pattern legs.

VFR • 4

Sectional Scale 1:500,000	10 Nautical Miles			
10 Statute Miles				

Entering Nontowered Airport
Landing Pattern Intentions

" .... • **traffic** ....
Airport Name/City   UNICOM   *Who:* Make and Tail #

entering .... • ....
                L/R   Pattern Leg

at .... **feet** • **for runway** .... "
Altitude MSL or "Pattern Altitude"

Use the area below to map out your
landing pattern legs.

VFR • 4

Sectional Scale 1:500,000	10 Nautical Miles			

10 Statute Miles

Entering Nontowered Airport Landing Pattern Intentions

" .... • traffic ....
Airport Name/City   UNICOM   *Who:* Make and Tail #

entering .... • ....
         L/R   Pattern Leg

at .... feet • for runway .... "
Altitude MSL or "Pattern Altitude"

Use the area below to map out your landing pattern legs.

VFR • 4

Sectional Scale 1:500,000	10 Nautical Miles			

10 Statute Miles

SET VOR

.... **VOR**

       Airport Name/City

.... **Frequency**

       Transmit and Receive

.... • .... **Frequency**

     Transmit only   Receive only

Set "TO" or "FROM" ....

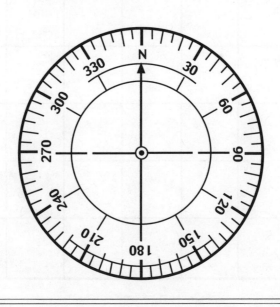

Sectional Scale 1:500,000	10 Nautical Miles				
10 Statute Miles					

SET VOR

.... **VOR**
　　　　Airport Name/City

.... **Frequency**
　　　　Transmit and Receive

.... • .... **Frequency**
　　Transmit only　　　　　　　　Receive only

Set "TO" or "FROM" ....

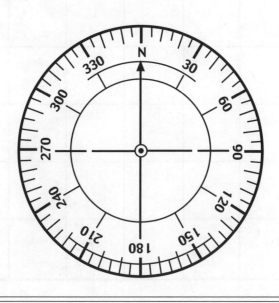

Sectional Scale 1:500,000	10 Nautical Miles				
10 Statute Miles					

SET VOR

.... **VOR**
Airport Name/City

.... **Frequency**
Transmit and Receive

.... • .... **Frequency**

Transmit only   Receive only

Set "TO" or "FROM" ....

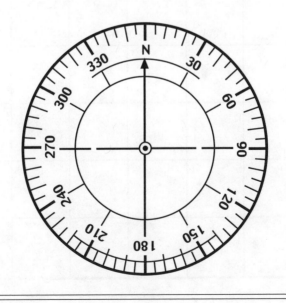

Sectional Scale 1:500,000	10 Nautical Miles			
10 Statute Miles				

SET VOR

.... **VOR**

Airport Name/City

.... **Frequency**

Transmit and Receive

.... • .... **Frequency**

Transmit only   Receive only

Set "TO" or "FROM" ....

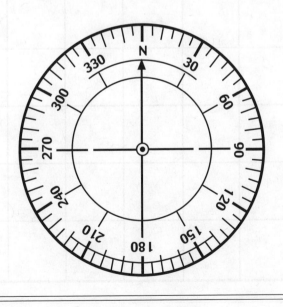

VFR • 5

Sectional Scale 1:500,000	10 Nautical Miles			
10 Statute Miles				

Activate Flight Plan

Tune radio to .... • ....

Frequency   Airport Name/City

OR

FSS telephone number ....

Pilot says:

"
.... **radio** ....

Airport Name/City   *Who:* Make and Tail #

listening on .... **at** .... **VOR or RCO."**

Frequency   Location

Flight Service Response:

"Go ahead .... **."**

Who: Make and Tail #

Pilot Response:

"
.... **radio, I wish to open**

Airport Name/City

my flight plan from ....

to .... **and to** .... **."**

Optional

Sectional Scale 1:500,000	10 Nautical Miles			
10 Statute Miles				

Activate Flight Plan

Tune radio to .... • ....
FrequencyAirport Name/City

—
OR
—

FSS telephone number ....

Pilot says:

"
.... **radio** ....
Airport Name/City *Who:* Make and Tail #

listening on .... **at** .... **VOR or RCO.**"
FrequencyLocation

Flight Service Response:

"**Go ahead** .... "
Who: Make and Tail #

Pilot Response:

"
.... **radio, I wish to open**
Airport Name/City

my flight plan from ....

to .... **and to** .... "
Optional

VFR • 6

Sectional Scale 1:500,000	10 Nautical Miles			
10 Statute Miles				

Activate Flight Plan

Tune radio to .... • ....

Frequency   Airport Name/City

OR

FSS telephone number ....

Pilot says:

"

.... **radio** ....

Airport Name/City   *Who:* Make and Tail #

listening on .... **at** .... **VOR or RCO.**"

Frequency   Location

Flight Service Response:

"**Go ahead** ...."

Who: Make and Tail #

Pilot Response:

"

.... **radio, I wish to open**

Airport Name/City

my flight plan from ....

to .... **and to** ...."

Optional

Sectional Scale 1:500,000	10 Nautical Miles			
10 Statute Miles				

Activate Flight Plan

Tune radio to .... • **...**

Frequency   Airport Name/City

―
OR
―

FSS telephone number ....

Pilot says:

"
.... radio ....

Airport Name/City   *Who:* Make and Tail #

listening on .... at .... VOR or RCO."

Frequency   Location

Flight Service Response:

"Go ahead ...."

Who: Make and Tail #

Pilot Response:

"
.. radio, I wish to open

Airport Name/City

my flight plan from ....

to .... and to ...."

            Optional

VFR • 6

Sectional Scale 1:500,000	10 Nautical Miles			
10 Statute Miles				

Close Flight Plan

Tune radio to .... • ....
Frequency   Airport Name/City

OR

FSS telephone number ....

Pilot says:

"

.... **radio** ....
Airport Name/City   *Who:* Make and Tail #

listening on .... **at** .... **VOR or RCO.** **"**
Frequency   Location

Flight Service Response:

"Go ahead .... **"** .
Who: Make and Tail #

Pilot Response:

"

.... **radio, I wish to close my**
Airport Name/City

flight plan from ....

to ....

and to .... **I have the airport in sight.** **"**
Optional

Sectional Scale 1:500,000	10 Nautical Miles				
10 Statute Miles					

Close Flight Plan

Tune radio to .... • ....
　　　　　　　　　Frequency　　　　　　　*Airport Name/City*

—
OR
—

FSS telephone number ....

Pilot says:

"
.... **radio** ....
　　　Airport Name/City　　　　　　　*Who:* Make and Tail #

listening on .... **at** .... **VOR or RCO."**
　　　　　　　Frequency　　　　　*Location*

Flight Service Response:

"Go ahead .... **."**
　　　　　　　　　Who: Make and Tail #

Pilot Response:

"
.... **radio, I wish to close my**
　　　　Airport Name/City

flight plan from ....

to ....

and to .... **. I have the airport in sight."**
　　　　　Optional

Sectional Scale 1:500,000	10 Nautical Miles				
10 Statute Miles					

Close Flight Plan

Tune radio to .... • ....
　　　　　　　　Frequency　　　　　　　Airport Name/City

OR

FSS telephone number ....

Pilot says:

"
.... **radio** ....
　Airport Name/City　　　　　　　*Who:* Make and Tail #

listening on .... **at** .... **VOR or RCO.**"
　　　　　　Frequency　　　　　Location

Flight Service Response:

"**Go ahead** ...."
　　　　　　　　　Who: Make and Tail #

Pilot Response:

"
.... **radio, I wish to close my**
　Airport Name/City

flight plan from ....

to ....

and to .... **I have the airport in sight.**"
　　　　Optional

Close Flight Plan　79

Sectional Scale 1:500,000	10 Nautical Miles			
10 Statute Miles				

Close Flight Plan

Tune radio to .... • ....

Frequency   Airport Name/City

OR

FSS telephone number ....

Pilot says:

"

.... **radio** ....

Airport Name/City   *Who:* Make and Tail #

listening on .... **at** .... **VOR or RCO."**

Frequency   Location

Flight Service Response:

"Go ahead .... **."**

Who: Make and Tail #

Pilot Response:

"

.... **radio, I wish to close my**

Airport Name/City

flight plan from ....

to ....

and to .... **. I have the airport in sight."**

Optional

VFR • 7

Sectional Scale 1:500,000	10 Nautical Miles			
10 Statute Miles				

Acquire ATIS, AWOS, or ASOS

.... **ATIS, AWOS, or ASOS** ....
Frequency   Airport Name/City

.... • .... • ....
Time   *Wind:* Dir/Speed/Gust   Temp/Dew

....
Sky Conditions

.... • .... • ....
Altimeter   Rwy(s) in Use   Rwy Freq.(s)

.... • ....
Density Altitude   Information Letter

....
Additional Information

....
NOTAMs

VFR • 8

Sectional Scale 1:500,000	10 Nautical Miles			
10 Statute Miles				

Acquire ATIS, AWOS, or ASOS

.... **ATIS, AWOS, or ASOS** ....
Frequency   Airport Name/City

.... • .... • ....
Time   *Wind:* Dir/Speed/Gust   Temp/Dew

....
Sky Conditions

.... • .... • ....
Altimeter   Rwy(s) in Use   Rwy Freq.(s)

.... • ....
Density Altitude   Information Letter

....
Additional Information

....
NOTAMs

Sectional Scale 1:500,000	10 Nautical Miles				
10 Statute Miles					

Acquire ATIS, AWOS, or ASOS

.... **ATIS, AWOS, or ASOS** ....
Frequency   Airport Name/City

.... ● .... ● ....
Time   *Wind:* Dir/Speed/Gust   Temp/Dew

....
Sky Conditions

.... ● .... ● ....
Altimeter   Rwy(s) in Use   Rwy Freq.(s)

.... ● ....
Density Altitude   Information Letter

....
Additional Information

....
NOTAMs

Sectional Scale 1:500,000	10 Nautical Miles				
10 Statute Miles					

Acquire ATIS, AWOS, or ASOS

·············· **ATIS, AWOS, or ASOS** ·····································
Frequency   Airport Name/City

····················· • ···································· • ·················
Time   *Wind:* Dir/Speed/Gust   Temp/Dew

··
Sky Conditions

····················· • ···································· • ·················
Altimeter   Rwy(s) in Use   Rwy Freq.(s)

································· • ·····································
Density Altitude   Information Letter

··
Additional Information

··
NOTAMs

VFR • 8

Sectional Scale 1:500,000	10 Nautical Miles			
10 Statute Miles				

Initial Approach Control Contact

Frequency .... **North Approach**

Frequency .... **South Approach**

Frequency .... **East Approach**

Frequency .... **West Approach**

Frequency .... • .... **Approach**
NW, NE, SW, SE

" .... **approach** ....
Airport Name/City   *Who:* Make and Tail #

.... • .... **at** .... **feet**
Where: Distance   Direction   Altitude MSL

inbound for ....
What: Stop and Go, Full Stop Landing, etc.

at ....
Optional: Satellite Airport Name/City

                                               "
with information ....
ATIS: Letter

....
Additional Information

Sectional Scale 1:500,000	10 Nautical Miles			
10 Statute Miles				

Initial Approach Control Contact

Frequency .... **North Approach**

Frequency .... **South Approach**

Frequency .... **East Approach**

Frequency .... **West Approach**

Frequency .... • .... **Approach**
                                         NW, NE, SW, SE

" .... **approach** ....
      Airport Name/City   *Who:* Make and Tail #

.... • .... **at** .... **feet**
Where: Distance   Direction   Altitude MSL

inbound for ....
                What: Stop and Go, Full Stop Landing, etc.

at ....
              Optional: Satellite Airport Name/City

with information .... **"** .
                     ATIS: Letter

....
                    Additional Information

Sectional Scale 1:500,000	10 Nautical Miles			
10 Statute Miles				

Initial Approach Control Contact

Frequency .... **North Approach**

Frequency .... **South Approach**

Frequency .... **East Approach**

Frequency .... **West Approach**

Frequency .... • .... **Approach**
                                        NW, NE, SW, SE

" .... **approach** ....
   Airport Name/City   *Who:* Make and Tail #

.... • .... **at** .... **feet**
Where: Distance   Direction   Altitude MSL

inbound for ....
                  What: Stop and Go, Full Stop Landing, etc.

at ....
              Optional: Satellite Airport Name/City

                                                              "
with information ....
                              ATIS: Letter

....
                   Additional Information

Sectional Scale 1:500,000	10 Nautical Miles			
10 Statute Miles				

Initial Approach Control Contact

Frequency .... **North Approach**

Frequency .... **South Approach**

Frequency .... **East Approach**

Frequency .... **West Approach**

Frequency .... • .... **Approach**
                                    NW, NE, SW, SE

"
.... **approach** ....
       Airport Name/City   *Who:* Make and Tail #

.... • .... **at** .... **feet**
Where: Distance   Direction   Altitude MSL

inbound for...
                        What: Stop and Go, Full Stop Landing, etc.

at... .
                  Optional: Satellite Airport Name/City

                                                                    "
with information.. .
                           ATIS: Letter

....
                    Additional Information

Sectional Scale 1:500,000	10 Nautical Miles			
10 Statute Miles				

Initial Approach Control
Class B Response

"**Remain clear of Class B airspace.**"

OR

"**Cleared to enter Class B airspace.**"

Followed by:

"**Squawk .... and IDENT.**"
                    Optional

"**Turn .... to heading ....**"
        L/R

AND/OR

"**Maintain, descend to, or ascend to .... feet**

for entering .... • **...**
                L/R   Pattern Leg

for runway ...."

AND/OR

"**Contact Tower at .... when**
                    Frequency

.... miles from the ...."
                    Airport, Midfield Downwind, etc.

Sectional Scale 1:500,000	10 Nautical Miles			
10 Statute Miles				

Initial Approach Control
Class B Response

"Remain clear of Class B airspace."

OR

"Cleared to enter Class B airspace."

Followed by:

"Squawk .... and IDENT."
                          Optional

"Turn .... to heading ...."
            L/R

AND/OR

"Maintain, descend to, or ascend to .... feet

for entering .... • ....
                L/R   Pattern Leg

for runway ...."

AND/OR

"Contact Tower at .... when
                      Frequency

.... miles from the ...."
                          Airport, Midfield Downwind, etc.

Sectional Scale 1:500,000	10 Nautical Miles			
10 Statute Miles				

Initial Approach Control
Class B Response

"Remain clear of Class B airspace."

OR

"Cleared to enter Class B airspace."

Followed by:

"Squawk .... **and IDENT."**
Optional

"Turn .... **to heading** .... **."**
L/R

AND/OR

"Maintain, descend to, or ascend to .... **feet**

for entering .... • ....
L/R   Pattern Leg

for runway .... **."**

AND/OR

"Contact Tower at .... **when**
Frequency

.... **miles from the** .... **."**
Airport, Midfield Downwind, etc.

Sectional Scale 1:500,000	10 Nautical Miles			
10 Statute Miles				

Initial Approach Control
Class B Response

"Remain clear of Class B airspace."

OR

"Cleared to enter Class B airspace."

Followed by:

"Squawk .... and IDENT."
                        Optional

"Turn .... to heading ...."
              L/R

AND/OR

"Maintain, descend to, or ascend to .... feet

for entering .... • ....
              L/R   Pattern Leg

for runway ...."

AND/OR

"Contact Tower at .... when
                        Frequency

.... miles from the ...."
                        Airport, Midfield Downwind, etc.

Sectional Scale 1:500,000	10 Nautical Miles			

10 Statute Miles

Initial Approach Control
Class C Response

"Squawk .... and IDENT."
Optional

"Maintain current heading."

OR

"Turn .... to heading ...."
       L/R

AND/OR

"Maintain, descend to, or ascend to .... feet

for entering .... • ....
       L/R   Pattern Leg

for runway ...."

AND/OR

"Contact Tower at .... when
                            Frequency

.... miles from the ...."
                                Airport, Midfield Downwind, etc.

VFR • 11

Sectional Scale 1:500,000	10 Nautical Miles			
10 Statute Miles				

Initial Approach Control
Class C Response

"Squawk .... and IDENT."

Optional

"Maintain current heading."

OR

"Turn .... to heading ...."

       L/R

AND/OR

"Maintain, descend to, or ascend to .... feet

for entering .... • ....

        L/R   Pattern Leg

for runway ...."

AND/OR

"Contact Tower at .... when

                   Frequency

.... miles from the ...."

               Airport, Midfield Downwind, etc.

Sectional Scale 1:500,000	10 Nautical Miles			
10 Statute Miles				

Initial Approach Control
Class C Response

"Squawk .... and IDENT."
Optional

"Maintain current heading."

OR

"Turn .... to heading ...."

L/R

AND/OR

"Maintain, descend to, or ascend to .... feet

for entering .... • ....

L/R   Pattern Leg

for runway ...."

AND/OR

"Contact Tower at .... when

Frequency

.... miles from the ...."

Airport, Midfield Downwind, etc.

Sectional Scale 1:500,000	10 Nautical Miles			
10 Statute Miles				

Initial Approach Control
Class C Response

"Squawk .... and IDENT."

Optional

"Maintain current heading."

—

OR

—

"Turn .... to heading ...."

L/R

AND/OR

"Maintain, descend to, or ascend to .... feet

for entering .... • ....

L/R   Pattern Leg

for runway ...."

AND/OR

"Contact Tower at .... when

Frequency

.... miles from the ...."

Airport, Midfield Downwind, etc.

Sectional Scale 1:500,000	10 Nautical Miles				
10 Statute Miles					

Initial Tower Contact/Response
After Using Approach Control

.... • .... •
Frequency   Runway

.... • .... • ....
Frequency   Runway   Airport Name/City

" .... **tower** .... •
Airport Name/City   *Who:* Make and Tail #

.... • .... **at** .... **feet**
Where: Distance   Direction   Altitude

Necessary for Class D, optional for Class B or Class C airspace:

inbound for entering .... • ....
                  L/R   Pattern Leg

for runway ....

---

for .... " .
        Options: Full Stop Landing, Touch and Go, etc.

Tower Response:

" .... **cleared for** ....
Who: Make and Tail #   L/R

.... **landing on runway** .... " .
Pattern Leg

Or " .... " .

VFR·12

Sectional Scale 1:500,000	10 Nautical Miles			
10 Statute Miles				

Initial Tower Contact/Response
After Using Approach Control

.... • .... •
Frequency   Runway

.... • .... • ....
Frequency   Runway   Airport Name/City

"
.... **tower** .... •
Airport Name/City   *Who:* Make and Tail #

.... • .... **at** .... **feet**
Where: Distance   Direction   Altitude

Necessary for Class D, optional for Class B or Class C airspace:

inbound for entering .... • ....
                                    L/R   Pattern Leg

for runway ....

---

for .... "
          Options: Full Stop Landing, Touch and Go, etc.

Tower Response:

"
.... **cleared for** ....
Who: Make and Tail #   L/R

.... **landing on runway** .... "
      Pattern Leg

Or " .... "

Sectional Scale 1:500,000	10 Nautical Miles			
10 Statute Miles				

Initial Tower Contact/Response
After Using Approach Control

.... • .... •
Frequency   Runway

.... • .... • ....
Frequency   Runway   Airport Name/City

" .... **tower** .... •
Airport Name/City   *Who:* Make and Tail #

.... • .... **at** .... **feet**
Where: Distance   Direction   Altitude

Necessary for Class D, optional for Class B or Class C airspace:

inbound for entering .... • ....
                       L/R   Pattern Leg

for runway ....

---

for ....**"** .
        Options: Full Stop Landing, Touch and Go, etc.

Tower Response:

" .... **cleared for** ....
Who: Make and Tail #   L/R

.... **landing on runway** ....**"** .
Pattern Leg

Or **"** ....**"** .

VFR · 12

Sectional Scale 1:500,000	10 Nautical Miles			
10 Statute Miles				

Initial Tower Contact/Response
After Using Approach Control

.... • .... •
Frequency   Runway

.... • .... • ....
Frequency   Runway   Airport Name/City

"
.... **tower** .... •
Airport Name/City   *Who:* Make and Tail #

.... • .... **at** .... **feet**
Where: Distance   Direction   Altitude

Necessary for Class D, optional for Class B or Class C airspace:

inbound for entering .... • ....
                              L/R   Pattern Leg

for runway ....

---

for .... **.**
          Options: Full Stop Landing, Touch and Go, etc.

Tower Response:

"
.... **cleared for** ....
Who: Make and Tail #   L/R

.... **landing on runway** .... **.**
Pattern Leg

Or " .... **.**

VFR • 12

Sectional Scale 1:500,000	10 Nautical Miles				
10 Statute Miles					

Initial Controlled Airport Without an Approach Control Contact

.... • ....
Frequency   Airport Name/City

"
.... **tower** .... •
Airport Name/City   *Who:* Make and Tail #

.... • .... **at** .... **feet**
Where: Distance   Direction   Altitude MSL

inbound for ....
What: Stop and Go, Full Stop Landing, etc.

"

with information ....
ATIS: Letter

....
Additional Information

VFR • 13

Sectional Scale 1:500,000	10 Nautical Miles			

10 Statute Miles

Initial Controlled Airport Without an Approach Control Contact

.... • ....
Frequency   Airport Name/City

"
.... **tower** .... •
Airport Name/City   *Who:* Make and Tail #

.... • .... **at** .... **feet**
Where: Distance   Direction   Altitude MSL

inbound for..
What: Stop and Go, Full Stop Landing, etc.

                                                                    "
with information.. .
ATIS: Letter

VFR • 13

....
Additional Information

Sectional Scale 1:500,000	10 Nautical Miles				
10 Statute Miles					

Initial Controlled Airport Without an Approach Control Contact

.... • ....

Frequency   Airport Name/City

" .... **tower** .... •

Airport Name/City   *Who:* Make and Tail #

.... • .... **at** .... **feet**

Where: Distance   Direction   Altitude MSL

inbound for..

What: Stop and Go, Full Stop Landing, etc.

with information... " .

ATIS: Letter

....

Additional Information

Sectional Scale 1:500,000	10 Nautical Miles			
10 Statute Miles				

Initial Controlled Airport Without an Approach Control Contact

.... • ....
Frequency   Airport Name/City

"
.... **tower** .... •
Airport Name/City   *Who:* Make and Tail #

.... • .... **at** .... **feet**
Where: Distance   Direction   Altitude MSL

inbound for ....
What: Stop and Go, Full Stop Landing, etc.

with information .... "
ATIS: Letter   .

....
Additional Information

Sectional Scale 1:500,000	10 Nautical Miles			
10 Statute Miles				

Initial Controlled Airport Without an Approach Control Response

"Squawk .... and IDENT."
Optional

AND/OR

"Suggest turn .... to heading ...."
          L/R

AND/OR

"Maintain, descend to, or ascend to .... feet

for entering .... • ....
            L/R   Pattern Leg

for runway ...."

AND/OR

"Contact Tower at ....
                        Frequency

when .... mile(s) from the

...."
           Airport, Midfield Downwind, etc.

VFR·14

Sectional Scale 1:500,000	10 Nautical Miles			
10 Statute Miles				

Initial Controlled Airport Without an Approach Control Response

"Squawk .... and IDENT."
                                                          Optional

---
AND/OR

"Suggest turn .... to heading ...."
              L/R

AND/OR

"Maintain, descend to, or ascend to .... feet

for entering .... • ....
              L/R   Pattern Leg

for runway ...."

AND/OR

"Contact Tower at ....
                                    Frequency

when .... mile(s) from the

....
              Airport, Midfield Downwind, etc.

VFR · 14

Sectional Scale 1:500,000	10 Nautical Miles			
10 Statute Miles				

Initial Controlled Airport Without an Approach Control Response

"Squawk .... and IDENT."
                                                              Optional

AND / OR

"Suggest turn .... to heading ...."
                        L/R

AND / OR

"Maintain, descend to, or ascend to .... feet

for entering .... • ....
                    L/R   Pattern Leg

for runway ...."

AND / OR

"Contact Tower at ....
                                        Frequency

when .... mile(s) from the

....
                Airport, Midfield Downwind, etc.

VFR • 14

Sectional Scale 1:500,000	10 Nautical Miles				
10 Statute Miles					

Initial Controlled Airport Without an Approach Control Response

"Squawk .... and IDENT."
Optional

AND/OR

"Suggest turn .... to heading ...."
    L/R

AND/OR

"Maintain, descend to, or ascend to .... feet

for entering .... • ....
           L/R   Pattern Leg

for runway ...."

AND/OR

"Contact Tower at ....
                              Frequency

when .... mile(s) from the

....
            Airport, Midfield Downwind, etc.

Sectional Scale 1:500,000	10 Nautical Miles				
10 Statute Miles					

Ground Control Taxi
After Landing Request

.... • ....
     Frequency   Airport Name/City

"
... Ground Control
                  Airport Name/City

....
Who: Make and Tail #

at .... and ....
             Runway   Taxiway

requests .... taxi
                   Direct, Progressive

                                                         "
instructions to ....
                  FBO or airport location

Use the area below to map out the
taxi path to your final stop on the airport grounds.

Sectional Scale 1:500,000	10 Nautical Miles			
10 Statute Miles				

Ground Control Taxi
After Landing Request

.... • ....
Frequency   Airport Name/City

"
.... **Ground Control**
Airport Name/City

....
Who: Make and Tail #

at .... **and** ....
Runway   Taxiway

requests .... **taxi**
Direct, Progressive

"
instructions to .... **.**
FBO or airport location

Use the area below to map out the
taxi path to your final stop on the airport grounds.

VFR • 15

Sectional Scale 1:500,000	10 Nautical Miles			
10 Statute Miles				

Ground Control Taxi
After Landing Request

.... • ....
     Frequency   Airport Name/City

"
.. Ground Control
              Airport Name/City

....
Who: Make and Tail #

at .... and ....
       Runway   Taxiway

requests .... taxi
                     Direct, Progressive

instructions to .... **"**
              FBO or airport location

Use the area below to map out the
taxi path to your final stop on the airport grounds.

VFR • 15

Sectional Scale 1:500,000	10 Nautical Miles			
10 Statute Miles				

Ground Control Taxi
After Landing Request

.... • ....
      Frequency   Airport Name/City

" .... **Ground Control**
                    Airport Name/City

....
Who: Make and Tail #

at .... **and** ....
          Runway   Taxiway

requests .... **taxi**
                    Direct, Progressive

                                          "
instructions to ....
                    FBO or airport location

Use the area below to map out the
taxi path to your final stop on the airport grounds.

Sectional Scale 1:500,000	10 Nautical Miles			
10 Statute Miles				

Clearance Delivery Contact

.... • ....
Frequency   Airport Name/City

"
.... **clearance delivery**
                   Airport Name/City

....
Who: Make and Tail #

requests instructions for VFR departure

to the .... • ....
     N, S, E, W   *Optional:* City

                                                              "
at .... **feet with information** ....
  Altitude MSL   ATIS: Letter

Sectional Scale 1:500,000	10 Nautical Miles			
10 Statute Miles				

Clearance Delivery Contact

.... • ....

Frequency   Airport Name/City

"

.. clearance delivery

Airport Name/City

....

Who: Make and Tail #

requests instructions for VFR departure

to the .... • ....

N, S, E, W   *Optional:* City

"

at .... feet with information ....

Altitude MSL   ATIS: Letter

VFR • 16

Sectional Scale 1:500,000	10 Nautical Miles			
10 Statute Miles				

Clearance Delivery Contact

.... • ....
        Frequency   Airport Name/City

"
.... **clearance delivery**
                Airport Name/City

....
                    Who: Make and Tail #

requests instructions for VFR departure

to the .... • ....
        N, S, E, W   *Optional:* City

"
at .... **feet with information** ....
    Altitude MSL   ATIS: Letter

Sectional Scale 1:500,000	10 Nautical Miles			
10 Statute Miles				

Clearance Delivery Contact

.... • ....
Frequency   Airport Name/City

"
.... **clearance delivery**
                   Airport Name/City

....
                        Who: Make and Tail #

requests instructions for VFR departure

to the .... • ....
                   N, S, E, W   *Optional:* City

"
at .... feet with information ....
       Altitude MSL   ATIS: Letter

VFR • 16

Sectional Scale 1:500,000	10 Nautical Miles			
10 Statute Miles				

Clearance Delivery Response

"
....
Who: Make and Tail #

Maintain VFR at or below .... **feet**

departure frequency will be ....
Frequency

squawk .... "

....
Additional Information

**Use the area below to sketch out your departure
path in the immediate vicinity of the airport.**

Sectional Scale 1:500,000	10 Nautical Miles			
10 Statute Miles				

Clearance Delivery Response

" ....
Who: Make and Tail #

Maintain VFR at or below .... **feet**

departure frequency will be ....
Frequency

squawk .... "

....
Additional Information

Use the area below to sketch out your departure path in the immediate vicinity of the airport.

Sectional Scale 1:500,000	10 Nautical Miles			
10 Statute Miles				

Clearance Delivery Response

"
....
Who: Make and Tail #

Maintain VFR at or below .... **feet**

departure frequency will be ....
Frequency

squawk .... **.** "

....
Additional Information

Use the area below to sketch out your departure path in the immediate vicinity of the airport.

Sectional Scale 1:500,000	10 Nautical Miles			
10 Statute Miles				

Clearance Delivery Response

"
....

Who: Make and Tail #

Maintain VFR at or below .... **feet**

departure frequency will be ....

Frequency

squawk .... "

....

Additional Information

**Use the area below to sketch out your departure
path in the immediate vicinity of the airport.**

Sectional Scale 1:500,000	10 Nautical Miles				
10 Statute Miles					

Ground Control Contact
When Ready to Depart

.... ● ....
      Frequency   Airport Name/City

"
.... **ground control**
                Airport Name/City

.... **requests**
         Who: Make and Tail #

.... **taxi instructions**
        Direct, Progressive

from .... **to the active**
         FBO or airport location, ramp, etc.

runway for VFR departure to the .... **."**
                              N, S, E, W

Sectional Scale 1:500,000	10 Nautical Miles			
10 Statute Miles				

Ground Control Contact
When Ready to Depart

.... • ....

Frequency   Airport Name/City

" .... **ground control**

Airport Name/City

.... **requests**

Who: Make and Tail #

.... **taxi instructions**

Direct, Progressive

from .... **to the active**

FBO or airport location, ramp, etc.

runway for VFR departure to the .... **."**

N, S, E, W

Sectional Scale 1:500,000	10 Nautical Miles			
10 Statute Miles				

Ground Control Contact
When Ready to Depart

.... • ....

Frequency   Airport Name/City

"

.... **ground control**

Airport Name/City

.... **requests**

Who: Make and Tail #

.... **taxi instructions**

Direct, Progressive

from .... **to the active**

FBO or airport location, ramp, etc.

runway for VFR departure to the .... **."**

N, S, E, W

Sectional Scale 1:500,000	10 Nautical Miles			
10 Statute Miles				

Ground Control Contact
When Ready to Depart

.... • ....
Frequency   Airport Name/City

"
.... **ground control**
                Airport Name/City

.... **requests**
            Who: Make and Tail #

.... **taxi instructions**
            Direct, Progressive

from .... **to the active**
                FBO or airport location, ramp, etc.

runway for VFR departure to the .... **."**
                                    N, S, E, W

Sectional Scale 1:500,000	10 Nautical Miles			
10 Statute Miles				

Ground Control Response to Your Departure Request

If direct route requested:

"
.... **taxi to runway** ....
Your make and tail #   Number

via taxiway ....

"
....
Additional directional instructions, if necessary

If progressive taxi requested:

"
.... **taxi to runway** ....
Your make and tail #   Number

turn .... **onto** ....
   L/R   Taxiway

and .... (Optional)

Now turn .... **onto** ....
    L/R   Taxiway

hold short of .... **at** .... "
  Runway or Taxiway   Runway or Taxiway

"**And** .... (Optional)

"
....
Additional directional instructions, if necessary

Sectional Scale 1:500,000	10 Nautical Miles			
10 Statute Miles				

Ground Control Response to Your Departure Request

If direct route requested:

" .... **taxi to runway** ....
　　　Your make and tail #　　　　　　　　　　　　　Number

via taxiway ....

　　　　　　　　　　　　　　　　　　　　　　　　　　　　　　　　　　"
....
Additional directional instructions, if necessary

If progressive taxi requested:

" .... **taxi to runway** ....
　　　Your make and tail #　　　　　　　　　　　　　Number

turn .... **onto** ....
　　　　　　　L/R　　　　　　　　　　Taxiway

and .... (Optional)

Now turn .... **onto** ....
　　　　　　　L/R　　　　　　　　Taxiway

　　　　　　　　　　　　　　　　　　　　　　　　　　　　　　　　"
hold short of .... **at** ....
　　　　　Runway or Taxiway　　　　　　Runway or Taxiway

".
And .... (Optional)

　　　　　　　　　　　　　　　　　　　　　　　　　　　　　　　　"
....
Additional directional instructions, if necessary

Sectional Scale 1:500,000	10 Nautical Miles			
10 Statute Miles				

Ground Control Response to Your Departure Request

VFR • 19

If direct route requested:

"

.... **taxi to runway** ....
Your make and tail #   Number

via taxiway ....

"
....
Additional directional instructions, if necessary

If progressive taxi requested:

"

.... **taxi to runway** ....
Your make and tail #   Number

turn .... **onto** ....
              L/R   Taxiway

and .... (Optional)

Now turn .... **onto** ....
                  L/R   Taxiway

                                                                        "
hold short of .... **at** ....
           Runway or Taxiway   Runway or Taxiway

"
And .... (Optional)

                                                                        "
....
Additional directional instructions, if necessary

Sectional Scale 1:500,000	10 Nautical Miles			
10 Statute Miles				

Ground Control Response to Your Departure Request

If direct route requested:

" .... **taxi to runway** ....

Your make and tail #   Number

via taxiway ....

.... "

Additional directional instructions, if necessary

If progressive taxi requested:

" .... **taxi to runway** ....

Your make and tail #   Number

turn .... **onto** ....

L/R   Taxiway

and .... (Optional)

Now turn .... **onto** ....

L/R   Taxiway

hold short of .... **at** .... "

Runway or Taxiway   Runway or Taxiway

" **And** .... (Optional)

.... "

Additional directional instructions, if necessary

Sectional Scale 1:500,000	10 Nautical Miles			
10 Statute Miles				

Clearance Delivery via Ground Control Contact When Ready to Depart

.... • ....
Frequency   Airport Name/City

"
.... **ground control**
Airport Name/City

.... **requests**
Who: Make and Tail #

.... **taxi instructions**
Direct, Progressive

from .... **to the**
FBO or airport location, ramp, etc.

active runway for VFR departure to the .... •
N, S, E, W

"

with information .... **.**
ATIS: Letter

VFR • 20

Sectional Scale 1:500,000	10 Nautical Miles			
10 Statute Miles				

Clearance Delivery via Ground Control Contact When Ready to Depart

.... • ....

Frequency   Airport Name/City

"

    .... **ground control**

            Airport Name/City

.... **requests**

            Who: Make and Tail #

.... **taxi instructions**

       Direct, Progressive

from .... **to the**

      FBO or airport location, ramp, etc.

active runway for VFR departure to the .... •

                          N, S, E, W

                                         "

with information .... **.**

                  ATIS: Letter

VFR • 20

Sectional Scale 1:500,000	10 Nautical Miles			
10 Statute Miles				

Clearance Delivery via Ground Control Contact When Ready to Depart

.... • ....
Frequency   Airport Name/City

" .... **ground control**
Airport Name/City

.... **requests**
Who: Make and Tail #

.... **taxi instructions**
Direct, Progressive

from .... **to the**
FBO or airport location, ramp, etc.

active runway for VFR departure to the .... •
N, S, E, W

with information .... " .
ATIS: Letter

Sectional Scale 1:500,000	10 Nautical Miles			
10 Statute Miles				

Clearance Delivery via Ground Control Contact When Ready to Depart

.... • ....
Frequency   Airport Name/City

" .... **ground control**
         Airport Name/City

.... **requests**
        Who: Make and Tail #

.... **taxi instructions**
        Direct, Progressive

from .... **to the**
        FBO or airport location, ramp, etc.

active runway for VFR departure to the .... •
                         N, S, E, W

                                                         "
with information ....
                    ATIS: Letter

VFR • 20

Sectional Scale 1:500,000	10 Nautical Miles			
10 Statute Miles				

Tower Contact When Ready to Depart

.... • .... •
Frequency   Runway

.... • .... • ....
Frequency   Runway   Airport Name/City

" .... **tower** ....
     Airport Name/City   *Who:* Make and Tail #

at .... **and** ....
       Runway   Taxiway

ready for VFR departure to the .... **."**
                                             N, S, E, W

**Use the area below to sketch out your departure
path in the immediate vicinity of the airport.**

VFR • 21

Sectional Scale 1:500,000	10 Nautical Miles			
10 Statute Miles				

Tower Contact When Ready to Depart

.... • .... •

Frequency   Runway

.... • .... • ....

Frequency   Runway   Airport Name/City

"

.... **tower** ....

Airport Name/City   *Who:* Make and Tail #

at .... **and** ....

Runway   Taxiway

"

ready for VFR departure to the ....

N, S, E, W

Use the area below to sketch out your departure path in the immediate vicinity of the airport.

Sectional Scale 1:500,000	10 Nautical Miles			
10 Statute Miles				

Tower Contact When Ready to Depart

.... • .... •

Frequency   Runway

.... • .... • ....

Frequency   Runway   Airport Name/City

"
.... **tower** ....

Airport Name/City   *Who:* Make and Tail #

at .... **and** ....

Runway   Taxiway

ready for VFR departure to the .... "

N, S, E, W

Use the area below to sketch out your departure path in the immediate vicinity of the airport.

Sectional Scale 1:500,000	10 Nautical Miles			
10 Statute Miles				

Tower Contact When Ready to Depart

.... • .... •

  Frequency   Runway

.... • .... • ....

  Frequency   Runway   Airport Name/City

"
.... **tower** ....

  Airport Name/City   *Who:* Make and Tail #

at .... **and** ....

  Runway   Taxiway

ready for VFR departure to the .... **.** "

  N, S, E, W

**Use the area below to sketch out your departure
path in the immediate vicinity of the airport.**

Sectional Scale 1:500,000	10 Nautical Miles			
10 Statute Miles				

Tower Response to Your Departure Request

Tower Response Choices:

"Hold short."

"Taxi into position and hold."

"Clear for takeoff."

One of the following choices may be added:

"Fly runway heading."

—
OR
—

"Turn to heading .... after reaching .... ft."
Altitude MSL

—
OR
—

"Fly runway heading until ...."
Optional

—
OR
—

"Contact Departure on ...."
Frequency

VFR · 22

Sectional Scale 1:500,000	10 Nautical Miles			
10 Statute Miles				

Tower Response to Your Departure Request

Tower Response Choices:

"Hold short."

"Taxi into position and hold."

"Clear for takeoff."

One of the following choices may be added:

"Fly runway heading."

─ OR ─

"Turn to heading .... after reaching .... ft."

Altitude MSL

─ OR ─

"Fly runway heading until ...."

Optional

─ OR ─

"Contact Departure on ...."

Frequency

VFR · 22

Sectional Scale 1:500,000	10 Nautical Miles			
10 Statute Miles				

Tower Response to Your Departure Request

Tower Response Choices:

"**Hold short.**"

"**Taxi into position and hold.**"

"**Clear for takeoff.**"

One of the following choices may be added:

"**Fly runway heading.**"

OR

"**Turn to heading .... after reaching .... ft.**"
Altitude MSL

OR

"**Fly runway heading until ....**"
Optional

OR

"**Contact Departure on ....**"
Frequency

VFR · 22

Sectional Scale 1:500,000	10 Nautical Miles			
10 Statute Miles				

Tower Response to Your Departure Request

Tower Response Choices:

"**Hold short.**"

"**Taxi into position and hold.**"

"**Clear for takeoff.**"

One of the following choices may be added:

"**Fly runway heading.**"

—
OR
—

"**Turn to heading .... after reaching .... ft.**"
Altitude MSL

—
OR
—

"**Fly runway heading until ....**"
Optional

—
OR
—

"**Contact Departure on ....**"
Frequency

VFR • 22

Sectional Scale 1:500,000	10 Nautical Miles			
10 Statute Miles				

Initial Departure Control Contact

Frequency .... **North Approach**

Frequency .... **South Approach**

Frequency .... **East Approach**

Frequency .... **West Approach**

Frequency .... • .... **Departure**
NW, NE, SW, SE

"
.... **departure** ....
Airport Name/City   *Who:* Make and Tail #

flying heading .... **requests**

VFR directions to the ....
Optional: **"Vectors"**   N, S, E, W, or Location

at .... **feet."**

VFR • 23

Sectional Scale 1:500,000	10 Nautical Miles			
10 Statute Miles				

Initial Departure Control Contact

Frequency .... North Approach

Frequency .... South Approach

Frequency .... East Approach

Frequency .... West Approach

Frequency .... • .... **Departure**
NW, NE, SW, SE

"
.... **departure** ....
Airport Name/City   *Who:* Make and Tail #

flying heading .... **requests**

VFR directions to the ....
Optional: **"Vectors"**   N, S, E, W, or Location

at .... **feet."**

Sectional Scale 1:500,000	10 Nautical Miles			
10 Statute Miles				

Initial Departure Control Contact

Frequency .... **North Approach**

Frequency .... **South Approach**

Frequency .... **East Approach**

Frequency .... **West Approach**

Frequency .... • .... **Departure**
NW, NE, SW, SE

"
.... **departure** ....
Airport Name/City   *Who:* Make and Tail #

flying heading .... **requests**

VFR directions to the ....
Optional: **"Vectors"**   N, S, E, W, or Location

at .... **feet."**

VFR · 23

Sectional Scale 1:500,000	10 Nautical Miles			
10 Statute Miles				

Initial Departure Control Contact

Frequency .... North Approach

Frequency .... South Approach

Frequency .... East Approach

Frequency .... West Approach

Frequency .... • .... Departure

NW, NE, SW, SE

" .... **departure** ....

Airport Name/City   *Who:* Make and Tail #

flying heading .... requests

VFR directions to the ....

Optional: "Vectors"   N, S, E, W, or Location

at .... feet.**"**

VFR · 23

Sectional Scale 1:500,000	10 Nautical Miles				
10 Statute Miles					

Initial Departure Control Response

"Squawk .... and IDENT."
Optional

AND/OR

"Fly heading .... •

maintain .... feet."
Altitude MSL

....
Additional directional instructions, if necessary

Departure Control's last communication will probably be:

".. radar service terminated.
Your Aircraft Make and Tail #

Tune transponder code ....

Resume your own navigation."

Pilot says:

"Resuming own navigation, thank you."

Sectional Scale 1:500,000	10 Nautical Miles			
10 Statute Miles				

Initial Departure Control Response

"Squawk .... and IDENT."
Optional

AND/OR

"Fly heading .... •

maintain .... feet."
Altitude MSL

....
Additional directional instructions, if necessary

Departure Control's last communication will probably be:

"... radar service terminated.
Your Aircraft Make and Tail #

Tune transponder code ....

Resume your own navigation."

Pilot says:

"Resuming own navigation, thank you."

VFR · 24

Sectional Scale 1:500,000	10 Nautical Miles			
10 Statute Miles				

Initial Departure Control Response

"Squawk .... and IDENT."
Optional

AND/OR

"Fly heading .... •

maintain .... feet."
Altitude MSL

....
Additional directional instructions, if necessary

Departure Control's last communication will probably be:

"
.... radar service terminated.
Your Aircraft Make and Tail #

Tune transponder code ....

Resume your own navigation."

Pilot says:

"Resuming own navigation, thank you."

VFR • 24

Sectional Scale 1:500,000	10 Nautical Miles			
10 Statute Miles				

Initial Departure Control Response

"Squawk .... and IDENT."
                                                          Optional

---
AND/OR

"Fly heading .... •

maintain .... feet."
                        Altitude MSL

....
        Additional directional instructions, if necessary

Departure Control's last communication will probably be:

"
.... radar service terminated.
    Your Aircraft Make and Tail #

Tune transponder code ....

Resume your own navigation."

Pilot says:

"Resuming own navigation, thank you."

Sectional Scale 1:500,000	10 Nautical Miles			
10 Statute Miles				

Transit MOA and/or
Restricted Area Contact

Frequency .... • .... **Approach/CTR**
Airport Name/City

Approach/Center phone number ....

" .... **approach/CTR** .... •
Airport Name/City   *Who:* Make and Tail #

.... • .... **of** ....
Where: Distance   Direction   City/Airport/Landmark, VOR

flying heading .... **at** .... **feet**
Altitude MSL

requests status of

**MOA(s) or
Restricted Area(s)** ....
ID Name

and (if necessary) ....
ID Name

and (if necessary) ....
ID Name

for permission to transit."

Sectional Scale 1:500,000	10 Nautical Miles			
10 Statute Miles				

Transit MOA and/or Restricted Area Contact

Frequency .... • .... **Approach/CTR**
Airport Name/City

Approach/Center phone number ....

"
.... **approach/CTR** .... •
Airport Name/City   *Who:* Make and Tail #

.... • .... **of** ....
Where: Distance   Direction   City/Airport/Landmark, VOR

flying heading .... **at** .... **feet**
                                      Altitude MSL

requests status of

**MOA(s) or
Restricted Area(s)** ....
                               ID Name

and (if necessary) ....
                             ID Name

and (if necessary) ....
                             ID Name

for permission to transit. "

Sectional Scale 1:500,000	10 Nautical Miles			
10 Statute Miles				

Transit MOA and/or Restricted Area Contact

Frequency .... • .... **Approach/CTR**
Airport Name/City

Approach/Center phone number ....

" .... **approach/CTR** .... •
Airport Name/City   *Who:* Make and Tail #

.... • .... **of** ....
Where: Distance   Direction   City/Airport/Landmark, VOR

flying heading .... **at** .... **feet**
Altitude MSL

requests status of

MOA(s) or
Restricted Area(s) ....
ID Name

and (if necessary) ....
ID Name

and (if necessary) ....
ID Name

for permission to transit."

Sectional Scale 1:500,000	10 Nautical Miles			
10 Statute Miles				

Transit MOA and/or Restricted Area Contact

Frequency .... • .... **Approach/CTR**
Airport Name/City

Approach/Center phone number ....

"
.... **approach/CTR** .... •
Airport Name/City   *Who:* Make and Tail #

.... • .... **of** ....
Where: Distance   Direction   City/Airport/Landmark, VOR

flying heading .... **at** .... **feet**
Altitude MSL

requests status of

**MOA(s) or
Restricted Area(s)** ....
ID Name

and (if necessary) ....
ID Name

and (if necessary) ....
ID Name

for permission to transit."

Sectional Scale 1:500,000	10 Nautical Miles			
10 Statute Miles				

Transit MOA and/or
Restricted Area Response

"Squawk .... **and IDENT."**

Optional

AND/OR

Name	Status	Altitude
(M) MOA or (R) Restricted Area	Hot or Cold (H) (C)	At or below MSL feet

Pilot Response: Optional

"

.... **approach/CTR** .... ●

Airport Name/City   *Who:* Make and Tail #

will monitor this frequency for the next

.... **minutes. Please notify if the area(s) status**

change(s)." ....

Sectional Scale 1:500,000	10 Nautical Miles				
10 Statute Miles					

Transit MOA and/or Restricted Area Response

"Squawk .... and IDENT."

Optional

__AND/OR__

Name	Status	Altitude
(M) MOA or (R) Restricted Area	Hot or Cold (H) (C)	At or below MSL feet

Pilot Response: Optional

"

.... approach/CTR .... •

Airport Name/City   *Who:* Make and Tail #

will monitor this frequency for the next

.... minutes. Please notify if the area(s) status

change(s)." ....

Sectional Scale 1:500,000	10 Nautical Miles				
10 Statute Miles					

Transit MOA and/or
Restricted Area Response

"Squawk .... and IDENT."

Optional

__AND/OR__

Name	Status	Altitude
(M) MOA or (R) Restricted Area	Hot or Cold (H) (C)	At or below MSL feet

Pilot Response: Optional

"

.... **approach/CTR** .... •

Airport Name/City   *Who:* Make and Tail #

will monitor this frequency for the next

.... **minutes. Please notify if the area(s) status**

change(s)." ....

Sectional Scale 1:500,000	10 Nautical Miles			
10 Statute Miles				

Transit MOA and/or Restricted Area Response

"Squawk .... **and IDENT."**

Optional

__AND/OR__

Name	Status	Altitude
(M) MOA or (R) Restricted Area	Hot or Cold (H) (C)	At or below MSL feet

Pilot Response: Optional

"

.... **approach/CTR** .... •

Airport Name/City   *Who:* Make and Tail #

will monitor this frequency for the next

.... **minutes. Please notify if the area(s) status**

change(s)." ....

Sectional Scale 1:500,000	10 Nautical Miles			
10 Statute Miles				

Flight Following Contact

Frequency .... • .... **Approach/CTR**
                       Airport Name/City

Approach/Center phone number ....

" .... **approach/CTR** .... •
Airport Name/City   *Who:* Make and Tail #

.... • .... **of** ....
Where: Distance   Direction   City/Airport/Landmark, VOR

flying heading .... **at** .... **feet**

requests FLIGHT FOLLOWING."

Sectional Scale 1:500,000	10 Nautical Miles			
10 Statute Miles				

Flight Following Contact

Frequency .... • .... **Approach/CTR**
        Airport Name/City

Approach/Center phone number ....

"
     .... **approach/CTR** .... •
   Airport Name/City   *Who:* Make and Tail #

.... • .... **of** ....
Where: Distance   Direction   City/Airport/Landmark, VOR

flying heading .... **at** .... **feet**

requests FLIGHT FOLLOWING."

Sectional Scale 1:500,000	10 Nautical Miles			
10 Statute Miles				

Flight Following Contact

Frequency .... • .... **Approach/CTR**

Airport Name/City

Approach/Center phone number ....

" .... **approach/CTR** .... •

Airport Name/City   *Who:* Make and Tail #

.... • .... **of** ....

Where: Distance   Direction   City/Airport/Landmark, VOR

flying heading .... **at** .... **feet**

requests FLIGHT FOLLOWING."

Sectional Scale 1:500,000	10 Nautical Miles				
10 Statute Miles					

Flight Following Contact

Frequency .... • .... **Approach/CTR**
Airport Name/City

Approach/Center phone number ....

"
.... **approach/CTR** .... •
Airport Name/City   *Who:* Make and Tail #

.... • .... **of** ....
Where: Distance   Direction   City/Airport/Landmark, VOR

flying heading .... **at** .... **feet**

requests FLIGHT FOLLOWING."

Sectional Scale 1:500,000	10 Nautical Miles			
10 Statute Miles				

Flight Following Response

"Can't approve request at this time."

OR

"Request approved."

"Traffic at .... o'clock

at, below, or above your attitude."

··

Additional Information

"Traffic at .... o'clock

at, below, or above your attitude."

··

Additional Information

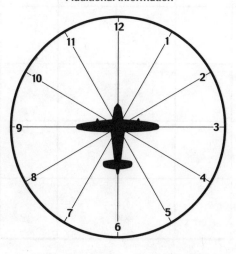

Sectional Scale 1:500,000	10 Nautical Miles			
10 Statute Miles				

Flight Following Response

"Can't approve request at this time."

OR

"Request approved."

"Traffic at .... o'clock

at, below, or above your attitude."

....
Additional Information

"Traffic at .... o'clock

at, below, or above your attitude."

....
Additional Information

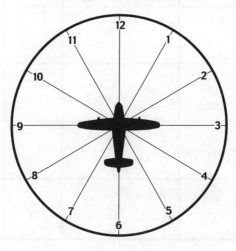

Sectional Scale 1:500,000	10 Nautical Miles			
10 Statute Miles				

Flight Following Response

"Can't approve request at this time."

OR

"Request approved."

"Traffic at .... o'clock

at, below, or above your attitude."

....
Additional Information

"Traffic at .... o'clock

at, below, or above your attitude."

....
Additional Information

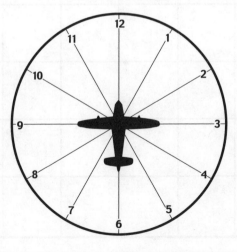

Sectional Scale 1:500,000	10 Nautical Miles			
10 Statute Miles				

Flight Following Response

"Can't approve request at this time."

OR

"Request approved."

"Traffic at .... o'clock

at, below, or above your attitude."

....
Additional Information

"Traffic at .... o'clock

at, below, or above your attitude."

....
Additional Information

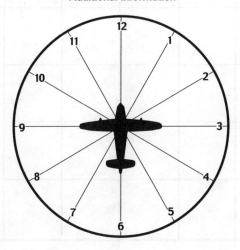

Sectional Scale 1:500,000	10 Nautical Miles			
10 Statute Miles				

General Purpose
Communication Template

Tune radio to ....
                    Frequency

" .... **Approach/Center/Radio/Traffic**
Who: Airport Name or City

....
Who: Make and Tail Number

.... **miles** ....
Where: Distance   Direction

from .... **at** ....
         Fix, NAVAID, Airport or Landmark   Altitude MSL

                                                        "
....
What: State Request or Announcement

Use this area for needed sketches.

Sectional Scale 1:500,000	10 Nautical Miles			
10 Statute Miles				

General Purpose
Communication Template

Tune radio to ....
                  Frequency

" .... Approach/Center/Radio/Traffic

Who: Airport Name or City

....

Who: Make and Tail Number

.... **miles** ....

Where: Distance   Direction

from .... **at** ....
        Fix, NAVAID, Airport or Landmark   Altitude MSL

                                                                    "
....

What: State Request or Announcement

Use this area for needed sketches.

VFR • 29

Sectional Scale 1:500,000	10 Nautical Miles			
10 Statute Miles				

General Purpose Communication Template

Tune radio to ....
                    Frequency

" .... **Approach/Center/Radio/Traffic**

Who: Airport Name or City

....

Who: Make and Tail Number

.... **miles** ....

Where: Distance   Direction

from .... **at** ....
       Fix, NAVAID, Airport or Landmark   Altitude MSL

                                                                    "
.... **.**

What: State Request or Announcement

Use this area for needed sketches.

Sectional Scale 1:500,000	10 Nautical Miles			
10 Statute Miles				

General Purpose
Communication Template

Tune radio to ....
                        Frequency

"
.... **Approach/Center/Radio/Traffic**

Who: Airport Name or City

....

Who: Make and Tail Number

.... **miles** ....

Where: Distance   Direction

from .... **at** ....
        Fix, NAVAID, Airport or Landmark   Altitude MSL

                                                            "
....

What: State Request or Announcement

Use this area for needed sketches.

Sectional Scale 1:500,000	10 Nautical Miles			
10 Statute Miles				

Communication Tips

Tip 1 The following format is generally used at initial call-up:

1. **WHO** you are calling.
2. **WHO** you are.
3. **WHERE** you are.
4. **WHAT** you want or what you are doing.

Tip 2 Be sure to pronounce numbers and letters correctly. Speak each word distinctly, at a speech rate of about 100 words a minute. Use the table below as a guide.

0 .... Zero	A .... Alpha	N ...... November
1 .... One	B .... Bravo	O .... October
2 .... Two	C .... Charlie	P .... Papa
3 .... Tree	D .... Delta	Q .... Quebec
4 .... Fore	E .... Echo	R .... Romeo
5 .... Fife	F .... Foxtrot	S .... Sierra
6 .... Six	G .... Golf	T .... Tango
7 .... Seven	H .... Hotel	U .... Uniform
8 .... Eight	I .... India	V .... Victor
9 .... Nin-er	J .... Juliet	W .... Whiskey
	K .... Kilo	X .... X-Ray
	L .... Lima	Y .... Yankee
	M ....Mike	Z .... Zulu

VFR · 30

Tip 3 When pronouncing numbers, use the digit format for numbers less than four digits, and the group format for numbers with four or more.

Examples

93 is said *Nin-er Tree*
138 is said *One Tree Eight*
9500 is said *Nin-er Thousand Fife Hundred*
1050 is said *One Thousand Fifty* or *Ten Fifty*
14500 is said *One Four Thousand Fife Hundred*

Sectional Scale 1:500,000	10 Nautical Miles			
10 Statute Miles				

Communication Tips

Tip 1   The following format is generally used at initial call-up:

1. **WHO** you are calling.
2. **WHO** you are.
3. **WHERE** you are.
4. **WHAT** you want or what you are doing.

Tip 2   Be sure to pronounce numbers and letters correctly. Speak each word distinctly, at a speech rate of about 100 words a minute. Use the table below as a guide.

0 .... Zero	A .... Alpha	N ...... November
1 .... One	B .... Bravo	O .... October
2 ....Two	C .... Charlie	P .... Papa
3 .... Tree	D .... Delta	Q .... Quebec
4 .... Fore	E .... Echo	R .... Romeo
5 .... Fife	F .... Foxtrot	S .... Sierra
6 .... Six	G ....Golf	T .... Tango
7 .... Seven	H .... Hotel	U .... Uniform
8 .... Eight	I .... India	V .... Victor
9 .... Nin-er	J .... Juliet	W .... Whiskey
	K .... Kilo	X .... X-Ray
	L .... Lima	Y .... Yankee
	M ....Mike	Z .... Zulu

Tip 3   When pronouncing numbers, use the digit format for numbers less than four digits, and the group format for numbers with four or more.

Examples

93 is said *Nin-er Tree*
138 is said *One Tree Eight*
9500 is said *Nin-er Thousand Fife Hundred*
1050 is said *One Thousand Fifty* or *Ten Fifty*
14500 is said *One Four Thousand Fife Hundred*

VFR • 30

Sectional Scale 1:500,000	10 Nautical Miles			
10 Statute Miles				

Communications Without a Radio

In the air:
1. Squawk 7600 (loss of radio) on your transponder.
2. Determine the airport landing patterns.
3. Enter the pattern at a 45° angle to the downwind leg.
4. Turn on your navigation and beacon lights.
5a. **Daytime:** Rock your wings and watch for the Tower's light signals.
5b. **Nighttime:** Flash landing lights and watch for the Tower's light signals.

On the ground:
1. Watch for other taxing aircraft.
2. Flash landing lights.
3. Watch for the Tower's light signals.

Color and Type of Signal	On The Gound	In Flight
	Meaning	
Steady Green	Cleared for takeoff	Cleared to land
Flashing Green	Cleared to taxi	Return for landing (to be followed by a steady green at proper time)
Steady Red	STOP!	Give way to other aircraft and continue circling
Flashing Red	Taxi clear of the landing area (runway) in use	Airport unsafe! DO NOT LAND!
Flashing White	Return to your starting point on airport	No assigned meaning
Alternating Red and Green	Exercise extreme caution	Exercise extreme caution

VFR • 31

Sectional Scale 1:500,000	10 Nautical Miles			
10 Statute Miles				

Communications Without a Radio

In the air:

1. Squawk 7600 (loss of radio) on your transponder.
2. Determine the airport landing patterns.
3. Enter the pattern at a 45° angle to the downwind leg.
4. Turn on your navigation and beacon lights.
5a. **Daytime:** Rock your wings and watch for the Tower's light signals.
5b. **Nighttime:** Flash landing lights and watch for the Tower's light signals.

On the ground:

1. Watch for other taxing aircraft.
2. Flash landing lights.
3. Watch for the Tower's light signals.

Color and Type of Signal	On The Gound	In Flight
	Meaning	
Steady Green	Cleared for takeoff	Cleared to land
Flashing Green	Cleared to taxi	Return for landing (to be followed by a steady green at proper time)
Steady Red	STOP!	Give way to other aircraft and continue circling
Flashing Red	Taxi clear of the landing area (runway) in use	Airport unsafe! DO NOT LAND!
Flashing White	Return to your starting point on airport	No assigned meaning
Alternating Red and Green	Exercise extreme caution	Exercise extreme caution

VFR · 31

Sectional Scale 1:500,000	10 Nautical Miles			
10 Statute Miles				

Emergency Communications

Stay calm.
Aviate • Navigate • Communicate

1. **Set** your transponder to:
   - 7700 for a mechanical, powerplant or electrical problem,
   - 7600 for a radio problem,
   - 7500 for a hijacking situation.

2. **Set** your radio to the emergency frequency **121.5** or
   call on your current frequency ....

3. **Say "Mayday, Mayday, Mayday.**

....
Who: Make and Tail #

.... **miles** ....
Number   *Where:* N, S, E, W

of ....
Location, Landmark, or Checkpoint

with .... souls on board at .... feet
Number   Altitude MSL

"
....
Problem

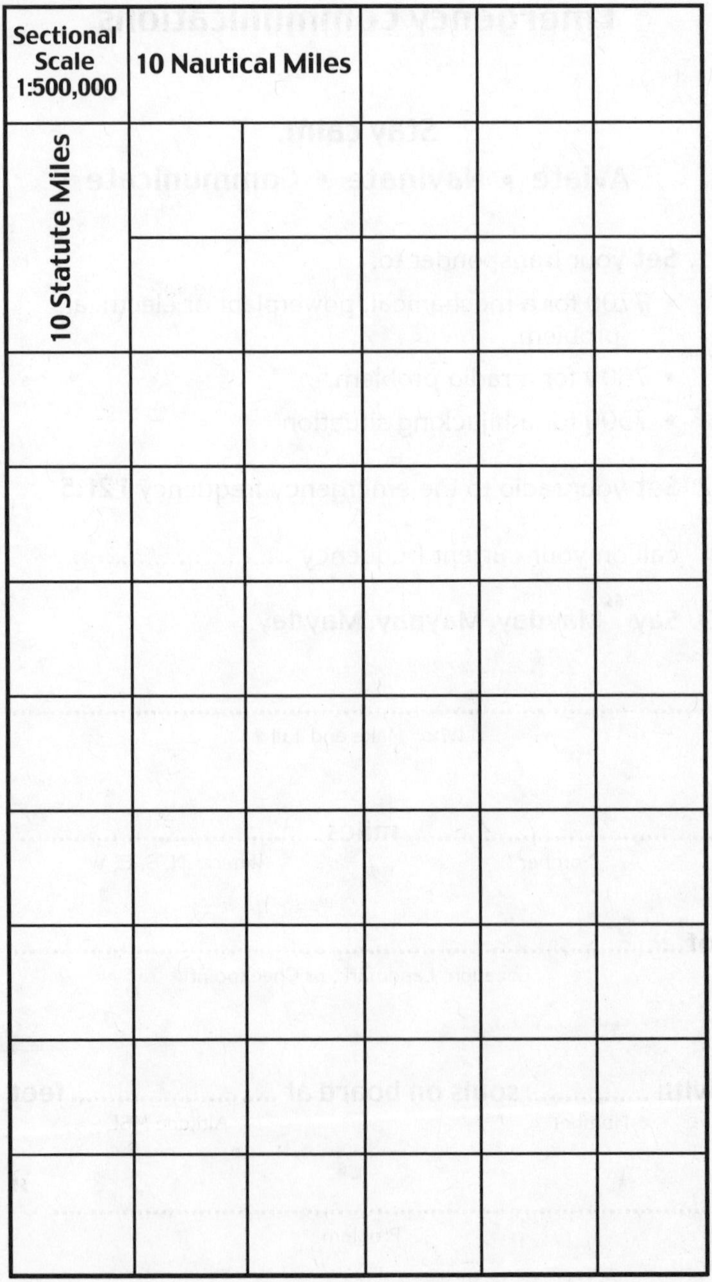
Sectional Scale 1:500,000
10 Nautical Miles
10 Statute Miles

Emergency Communications

Stay calm.
Aviate • Navigate • Communicate

1. **Set** your transponder to:
   - 7700 for a mechanical, powerplant or electrical problem,
   - 7600 for a radio problem,
   - 7500 for a hijacking situation.

2. **Set** your radio to the emergency frequency **121.5** or
   call on your current frequency ....

3. **Say** "**Mayday, Mayday, Mayday**.

....
Who: Make and Tail #

.... **miles** ....
Number   *Where:* N, S, E, W

of..
Location, Landmark, or Checkpoint

with .... **souls on board at** .... **feet**
Number   Altitude MSL

"
....
Problem

VFR • 32

Sectional Scale 1:500,000	10 Nautical Miles			
10 Statute Miles				

Acknowledgments

Clear, simple, and understandable communications between aircraft pilots in flight, and between an aircraft pilot and ATC (Air Traffic Control), are vital to the safe skies we enjoy. Unfortunately, the process to *become* and *stay* a competent and efficient VFR (Visual Flight Rules) communicator is fraught with many challenges. Without a clear and deeply rooted understanding of the necessary communication protocols in all types of airspace and timely and consistent practice, student pilots quit, and pilots who haven't kept themselves current never come back. The task of VFR communicating sadly keeps too many people from completing their private pilot's license and it keeps inactive pilots from renewing their life long interest in flying.

Thanks go to the personnel of the ATCs at Daytona Beach and Sanford, Florida airports for answering many of my questions and giving me the encouragement to continue my research about the correct phraseology of VFR communications. Additional thanks must go to James Guildi, Carl Barden and Ben McKee during my pilot training. Their patience made a big difference in my "staying the course."

The templates in this book are the result of utilizing the experiences of many people and information garnered from many official resources such as the regulations and AIM, to name just a few. The book has been made available to the general aviation community so that it can help anyone who desires to *become* and *stay* proficient and effective under VFR communication conditions. I sincerely believe that once users are competent with their VFR communication skills, they will fly more often, and through the joy of flying, each one may be able to "put out [his or her] hand and [touch] the face of God."[1]

---

[1] Magee Jr., John Gillespie, *High Flight*, New York: New York Times Herald, September 3, 1942